PLAYING WITH FIRE
Stories from the Pacific Rim

These stories come from different countries and islands around the Pacific Ocean. The people in the stories are all different, except for one thing – they all play with fire, take risks, do foolish or dangerous things . . . Ole, a quiet shy man, learns to play the game of development aid and becomes a man of the world. Maggie, an unhappy mother, is living on the edge of misery, even madness. An honest, hard-working government clerk like Marina just wants her promotion and her pay increase – how could she know that men could be so greedy, so cruel? Little Avusi is scared of ghosts and keeps his eyes shut, while Tuaine, sent away from home to school in New Zealand, has no friends or family to help her in her time of need . . .

BOOKWORMS WORLD STORIES

English has become an international language, and is used on every continent, in many varieties, for all kinds of purposes. *Bookworms World Stories* are the latest addition to the Oxford Bookworms Library. Their aim is to bring the best of the world's stories to the English language learner, and to celebrate the use of English for storytelling all around the world.

Jennifer Bassett
Series Editor

D1568859

OXFORD BOOKWORMS LIBRARY

World Stories

Playing with Fire

Stories from the Pacific Rim

Stage 3 (1000 headwords)

Series Editor: Jennifer Bassett
Founder Editor: Tricia Hedge
Activities Editors: Jennifer Bassett and Christine Lindop

NOTES ON THE ILLUSTRATORS

JENNIFER LAUTUSI (illustrations on pages 4, 9, 13, 56) lives in Christchurch, New Zealand, and has illustrated more children's books than she can remember. She lived in Western Samoa for three years, where she still has family links, and specialises in drawing Pacific Island people. She is one of New Zealand's best-known illustrators, and her illustrations have won many prizes.

JO THAPA (illustration on page 18) lives in Wellington, New Zealand, with her partner, cat, dog, and two birds. She is an illustrator and a painter, working in both digital and traditional painted mediums. She exhibits her paintings regularly in Wellington.

ROMEO CASTILLO MANANQUIL (illustrations on pages 24, 30, 35) was born in the Philippines and was an honor graduate in Fine Arts at the University of the Philippines. He soon became an award-winning illustrator for books and magazines, and later designed for the Central Bank of the Philippines a series of bank notes and coins, which included the 1000-peso bill still in circulation. He is also a painter and portraitist. MananQuil now lives in Canada with his family, and is known as one of the leading Filipino artists in Canada today.

THERESA REIHANA (illustrations on pages 41, 46, 50) is of mixed heritage, both Māori and European, and her Iwi or tribe is Ngatihine and Ngapuhi. She was brought up in the multi-cultural society of Auckland and spent most of her adult life as a truck driver and labourer. A mother of six, she now lives in the far north of her homeland New Zealand, and is a well-known contemporary Māori artist. Reihana has had exhibitions of her work in Italy, Australia, and all over New Zealand.

RETOLD BY JENNIFER BASSETT

Playing with Fire

Stories from the Pacific Rim

OXFORD UNIVERSITY PRESS

Distributed By:
Grass Roots Press
Toll Free: 1-888-303-3213
Fax: (780) 413-6582
Web Site: www.grassrootsbooks.net

OXFORD

UNIVERSITY PRESS

Great Clarendon Street, Oxford OX2 6DP

Oxford University Press is a department of the University of Oxford.
It furthers the University's objective of excellence in research, scholarship,
and education by publishing worldwide in

Oxford New York

Auckland Cape Town Dar es Salaam Hong Kong Karachi
Kuala Lumpur Madrid Melbourne Mexico City Nairobi
New Delhi Shanghai Taipei Toronto

With offices in

Argentina Austria Brazil Chile Czech Republic France Greece
Guatemala Hungary Italy Japan Poland Portugal Singapore
South Korea Switzerland Thailand Turkey Ukraine Vietnam

OXFORD and OXFORD ENGLISH are registered trade marks of
Oxford University Press in the UK and in certain other countries

ISBN: 978 0 19 479284 4

A complete recording of this Bookworms edition of
Playing with Fire: Stories from the Pacific Rim is available on
audio CD ISBN 978 0 19 479285 1

Printed in Hong Kong

ACKNOWLEDGEMENTS

*The publishers are grateful to the following for permission to adapt and
simplify copyright texts*: Epeli Hau'ofa for *The Glorious Pacific Way*;
Denise Whittaker for *Maggie*; the author for *Progress* from *Waywaya and Other Stories*
by F. Sionil José; David A. Kulu for *My Little Ghost*; Graeme Lay for *The Jacket*

Illustrations by: Jennifer Lautusi (pp 4, 9, 13, 56), Romeo Castillo MananQuil
(pp 24, 30, 35), Theresa Reihana (pp 41, 46, 50), Jo Thapa (pp 18)

Word count (main text): 12,589 words

For more information on the Oxford Bookworms Library,
visit www.oup.com/bookworms

CONTENTS

INTRODUCTION   i

NOTES ON THE ILLUSTRATORS   iv

NOTE ON THE LANGUAGE   viii

TONGA

The Glorious Pacific Way *Epeli Hau'ofa*   1

NEW ZEALAND

Maggie *Denise Whittaker*   16

PHILIPPINES

Progress *F. Sionil José*   20

NEW ZEALAND

The Jacket *Graeme Lay*   37

PAPUA NEW GUINEA

My Little Ghost *David A. Kulu*   54

GLOSSARY   58

ACTIVITIES: Before Reading   61

ACTIVITIES: After Reading   63

ABOUT THE AUTHORS   67

ABOUT THE BOOKWORMS LIBRARY   70

NOTE ON THE LANGUAGE

There are many varieties of English spoken in the world, and the characters in these stories sometimes use non-standard forms. This is how the authors of the original stories represented the spoken language that their characters would actually use in real life. There are also words that are usually only found in a particular variety of English (for example, *bubu* and *jeepney*). These words are either explained in the stories or in the glossary on page 58.

The Glorious Pacific Way

EPELI HAU'OFA

A story from Tonga, retold by Jennifer Bassett

In the South Pacific the history and beliefs of the people are told in stories that go back centuries. These stories are not written, but live as spoken words, passed on from parent to child, family to family, year after year.

In the modern world it is easy for oral traditions to be lost. Ole Pasifikiwei on the island of Tiko loves these old stories, so he writes them down. But it is slow work – it would be wonderful to have a typewriter . . .

'I hear you're collecting oral traditions. Good work,' said Mr Harold Minte. 'I'm pleased to hear that someone is writing down these old stories before they're lost for ever.'

Mr Minte was a diplomat. His voice was friendly, but he sounded like a teacher speaking to a schoolboy.

'Thank you, sir,' Ole Pasifikiwei said shyly. He was not usually shy, except with foreigners, but tonight he was at a drinks party for diplomats in the beautiful gardens of the International Nightlight Hotel, and he found conversation difficult.

Ole spent most of the free time from his job collecting

oral traditions. He felt that God was telling him to do this work, and it had become the great interest of his life.

He had begun by writing down his own family's history and stories, then went on to other families in the village, and then to neighbouring villages. In seven years he had covered a fifth of his island country. He wrote with a pen in notebooks, which he kept in a tall pile in a corner of his house. He hoped that one day he would have a typewriter and some filing cabinets to keep all the papers safe.

People at MERCY (the Ministry of Environment, Religion, Culture, and Youth) knew about Ole's work on oral traditions, and thought it was a very fine thing. A senior official in MERCY, who was also a good friend of Ole's, had invited him to the drinks party to meet Mr Minte, because Mr Minte was in Tiko to talk about development, and to find out where aid and money were needed.

'Perhaps some money will make your work easier,' Mr Minte said now to Ole.

'That'll help a lot, sir,' said Ole.

'We have development money especially for cultural projects like this. We want to make sure that the Pacific Way is not lost. We want to help you.'

'Very kind of you, sir. When can I have some money?'

'After you've written me a letter asking for aid.'

'Do I have to? Can't you just send some money?'

'You haven't done business with us before, have you?'

'No, sir.'

'Things are not as simple as that, you know. We have the money to give away, but first, you must ask us. Tell us what you want. *We* don't want to tell *you* what you should do. My job is to tell people that we want to work together, and people should ask us for help. Do you understand?'

'Yes, sir. But suppose no one asks?' said Ole.

'That's no problem. When people know they can get things from us for nothing, they will ask. Come and see me at ten tomorrow morning at the MERCY building. Think of what I've said and we'll talk about it then. I'm pleased we've met. Good night.'

Soon Ole left the party and went home, feeling worried and uncomfortable. He had never before asked for anything from a stranger. 'I'm not a beggar,' he thought. 'If Mr Minte has money to give away, why doesn't he just give it? Why must I beg for it?'

He began to have feelings of hate for Mr Minte. He needed a typewriter and some filing cabinets, not for himself, but for the important work he was doing. But he was too proud to ask for them. Was it wrong to be proud? Probably. It wasn't easy to ask for things from a stranger – but he had to do it because there was no other way of getting a typewriter and some filing cabinets.

'Oh, well,' he thought, as he lay in bed that night, 'it's like breaking the law, I suppose. After you've done it once, it just gets easier and easier.'

At ten the next morning Ole was at the MERCY building.

'Good morning, Ole,' said Mr Minte. 'Have you decided if you want help from us?'

'Yes, sir. I'd like to have a typewriter and some filing cabinets. I'll write you a letter. Thank you.'

'We don't want to tell people what to do with our money,'
said Mr Minte, 'but there are things that we cannot pay for.'

'Now, Ole, I'm afraid that's not possible. We don't want to tell people what to do with our money, but there are things that we cannot pay for. My Minister at home has to explain to the government how our development money is used. Why does a project about oral traditions in an island culture need a modern machine like a typewriter? No, no, the government won't like that at all!'

'But I need a typewriter because . . .'

'No, no, no,' Mr Minte said. 'You have to think again. What you ask for must *look* right, *feel* right for the project.'

He stopped for a moment. 'Look, we can give you 2,000 dollars a year for the next five years for a newsletter about your project. Publish a newsletter every month and send us one copy, OK?'

'But I still need a typewriter to publish a newsletter,' said Ole.

'Try using a MERCY typewriter. And you will have to have a committee, you know.'

'A committee? What for?' said Ole. 'I've worked alone for seven years, and no committee has been interested in me.'

'Oh, they will be, they will be, when they hear there is good development money. But we don't give to people, you see, only to committees. Get a group of people together, call them the Oral Traditions Committee or something, which will then write to us for help. Do you understand?' Mr Minte looked at his watch. 'I'm sorry, I have to go now to talk to the National Women's Organization. Your women are much better at starting committees than your men, you know. Their organizations get lots and lots of development money.

Think about it and come again tomorrow at the same time. See you then.'

Mr Minte went out and disappeared into a long shiny black car.

Ole stayed in the office, keeping very still and breathing deeply until he felt calmer. He always did this when he was angry. Finally, he got up and walked slowly to the office of his friend, Emi Bagarap, the senior MERCY official. Emi sat quietly and listened until Ole finished speaking.

'The trouble with you is that you're too honest,' Emi said. 'And too proud.'

'It's not being proud,' said Ole. 'It's self-respect.'

'Oh, self-respect is very fine, of course,' Emi said. 'But we can't afford it now. When our country is developed, then we can be proud and have lots of self-respect . . .'

'And suppose our country is never developed?' said Ole.

'We will develop!' said Emi. 'Of course we will. You have to believe that the future is full of hope for us. Remember that we're playing international games. The other players have the money, and we don't. Simple as that. They make the rules, and we try to make the rules work better for us. Look at Mr Minte. He offers you 2,000 dollars for five years, and he wants you to start a committee, then the committee writes a letter asking for funds and publishes a monthly newsletter. That's all. But he didn't say anything about what kind of committee, or who should be on it, did he? You can get three or four friends to be your committee. Get people who aren't very interested, and who don't know very much. Then you'll be free to do the things you need.

'And the letter will come from the committee, not from you yourself, so your self-respect will not be hurt in any way. Although that doesn't really matter, of course.

'Another thing. Mr Minte didn't say how long the newsletter should be, did he? You can write it in a page or two and it will take you about half an hour each month. And you don't have to write it in English. And if you wish, you can just publish two copies – one for you and one for Mr Minte. I'm not telling you to do this; that would be dishonest, you see. I'm only explaining to you one of the possible ways to play this game.

'And most importantly,' Emi continued, 'Mr Minte didn't say what you should do with the rest of the money. So. You pay perhaps two dollars a year for your newsletter, and with the rest of the money you can buy a typewriter and four filing cabinets every year for five years.

'You see, Mr Minte is very good and very kind; he's been playing international games for a long, long time and he understands the rules. He wants you to have your typewriter and the other things but won't say it. Go see him tomorrow and tell him you'll do what he told you.

'But remember that when you are doing business with foreigners, don't be too clever. It's better to look like a poor, grateful islander, who knows nothing. And you're too fat – try to get thinner. We need to look like poor, hungry people. The reason why Tiko gets very little aid money is because our people are too fat and happy. I wish our government would realize that and do something about it.'

And so, Emi Bagarap, who had put his own self-respect

away in a dark cupboard many years ago, taught his friend, the learner, the ways of the world.

When Ole left the office, he felt much less worried – almost happy, in fact. He had begun to understand some of life's many problems. 'Give me time, dear God,' he thought as he walked towards the bus stop, 'and I will become an excellent player of this game.'

'A word with you, old friend,' Manu's voice stopped him.

'Oh, hello, Manu,' Ole said. 'Long time no see. Where have you been?'

'Watching you, old friend. You have that look on your face,' Manu said simply.

'What look?' asked Ole, not understanding.

'The look of someone who's been listening to people like Emi Bagarap. I'm worried about you. I must tell you before it's too late. Don't let Emi or people like him persuade you to do something you—'

'I never let anyone persuade me to do anything that I don't want to do,' said Ole, very crossly.

'It's already happened, old friend; it's written all over your face. Be careful of Emi. He has sold his soul, and will make you sell yours if you're not careful.'

'That's stupid. No one has sold his soul,' said Ole. 'We're just being sensible, until we get what's good for the country.'

'No, no, old friend. You are selling your soul. And you'll never get it back because you will not want to.'

'I don't have time for this, Manu. You belong to the past; it's time to wake up to the future.' And with those sharp words Ole walked quickly away.

'I never let anyone persuade me to do anything that I don't want to do,' said Ole, very crossly.

Next day when he met Mr Minte he was all smiles. The diplomat saw the change in Ole, and gave a smooth little smile in return. He had seen this change many times before. It was part of his job to make this change happen.

'So, Ole, when will you start the committee?'

'Tonight, sir.'

'Well done, Mr Chairman. If your secretary writes me a letter, you'll get your first 2,000 dollars in a month's time.'

'Thank you very much, Mr Minte. I'm most grateful.'

'You're welcome. I've enjoyed doing business with you, Ole. You have a great future. If you need anything, just tell me. You know, the Pacific needs more people like you. Then these countries would develop faster than the speed of light.'

They shook hands, and as Ole opened the door, Mr Minte called out, 'Ah yes, there will soon be a training course in Manila on collecting oral traditions. You should go; it will be good for you. I'll let you know in a few weeks.'

'Thank you again, Mr Minte.'

'Don't mention it. I'm always happy to help. Goodbye for now. I hope you'll soon get a typewriter and filing cabinets.'

Ole sang quietly to himself on the way home, very happy. That evening the Committee for the Collection of Oral Traditions was born. Ole was the chairman, his youngest brother was the secretary, and three friends became committee members. The Committee began work immediately and wrote a letter to Mr Minte which was taken to the MERCY building the next day. A month later Ole received a cheque for 2,000 dollars and a letter inviting him to go on a six-week training course in Manila. He went, leaving his house in the care of his old aunt, who did not understand what he was doing.

He found the training course hard to understand, and the night-life in Manila was much more exciting. In fact, Ole had a very enjoyable time indeed, and in the third week he had to visit a doctor, who was most kind and understanding, and gave Ole the necessary medicine.

On his way home Ole bought a typewriter in Sydney airport, and also ordered four filing cabinets, which would come to the island by ship. He was very pleased. His dream was coming true, and so quickly! As his plane landed at Tiko airport, he saw himself in the future – the head, no, the President of the National Committee for Island Culture.

When he finally arrived home, his old aunt greeted him with tears of happiness.

'Ole, Ole, you're safe. Thank God those foreigners didn't eat you. You look so thin; what did they do to you?'

'Don't worry, auntie,' Ole laughed. 'Those foreigners don't eat people. They only shoot each other.'

'You look so sick. Did they try to shoot you too?'

'I'm very healthy.' Ole laughed, remembering his night-life adventures in Manila.

'What's the matter, Ole? Why are you laughing?'

'The house looks very tidy,' Ole said quickly. 'Thank you for taking care of it. You are always very good to me.'

'Oh, Ole, I cleaned the place from top to bottom,' said his aunt. 'You need a wife to clean up after you. Why don't you get married? You were always untidy, and you haven't changed. I threw out so much rubbish from your house.'

These words began to worry Ole a little.

'You did, did you? And what did you do with my books?'

'Books? What books?'

'Those notebooks in the pile in the corner of the room.'

'You mean those dirty old school notebooks? They had all kinds of insects living in them, Ole.'

'They're the most important things in my life,' said Ole, and went looking for his books. 'They aren't here. What have you done with them?' he shouted.

'Sit down, Ole, and let's talk calmly.'

'No! Where are they?'

'Ole, you've always been a good boy. Sit down and have something to eat. You must be hungry.'

'Never mind that, I want my books!'

'Sit down and don't scream at me. That's a good boy. We're poor, you, me, the neighbours. Food is expensive.'

'Where are my books?'

'We can't afford toilet paper. It used to be ten cents.'

'Yes, but what about my books?'

'You didn't leave me any money when you went away, Ole. I had to eat, and keep clean. Things are so expensive.'

'I'm sorry, but where are my books?'

'Don't keep asking me that question, Ole. I'm trying to explain. I'm your only living aunt. And I'm very old, and ready to go to Heaven. Don't hurry me, please. Don't you think I'm more important than some old book?'

'What did you do with them? Where are they?'

'Ole, I had no money for food, no money for toilet paper. I had to eat and keep clean. Stop looking at me like that. You

'Those books are the most important things in my life.
What have you done with them?' Ole shouted.

frighten me.' She stopped, then went on very quietly. 'I used some and sold the rest cheaply to the neighbours. They're poor, Ole, but they also have to keep clean.'

Ole stared at his aunt. He could not believe it. 'No, no, you're just having some fun with me. You didn't really sell my books for toilet paper . . .'

'I did. Yes, yes, I did. I'm sorry, but I didn't know they were important. How could I know?'

'Oh, my God!'

Ole could not speak for a moment. He sat very still, breathing deeply. Then slowly, very slowly, he whispered, 'Seven years' hard work down the toilet; shit!'

Suddenly the meaning of the word 'shit' hit him, and he began laughing wildly, with tears running down his face. At the same moment the best idea of his life came to him.

He put his arms round his aunt and said he was sorry for being angry. The old lady was very surprised at this sudden change in him, and cried with happiness.

Ole remembered that Mr Minte's government had promised him 10,000 dollars over five years. That was the start. Ole Pasifikiwei, whose books had gone down the toilet, would now go fishing in the big seas.

'If I am a beggar,' he told himself, 'I will be a big beggar, a grand beggar, the best beggar of all.'

He wrote Mr Minte a letter, and not long afterwards Dr Andrew Wheeler arrived on the island. Dr Wheeler was a very clever man and knew all about development aid. With his help, Ole began a National Committee for Cultural Studies, and on the Committee he got chiefs, government ministers, VIPs, wives of VIPs, and his old friend, Emi Bagarap. He himself was full-time secretary. Then Dr Wheeler wrote a plan for a four-year project, and letters asking for 400,000 dollars in aid. The letters were sent to every organization which had aid funds to give away.

A little later, again with Dr Wheeler's help, Ole formed eighteen other national committees and organizations. They all had wonderfully necessary and important projects, which needed generous development aid. And after six years Ole had asked for 14 million dollars for his different committees. His name was now well known by all the important aid people in Brussels, The Hague, Bonn, Geneva, Paris, London, New York, Washington, Wellington, Canberra, Tokyo, Peking, and Moscow. The University of the Southern Paradise, recognizing what a great man Ole had become, gave him many grand titles.

Ole Pasifikiwei became an extraordinarily clever player of international aid games, enjoying every new rule and learning how to turn it upside-down and inside-out. His early worries about self-respect have disappeared, and he works hard at his full-time job of first-class, expert beggar.

Maggie

DENISE WHITTAKER

A story from New Zealand, retold by Jennifer Bassett

Can you imagine what it feels like to lose a child? Most of us can't imagine that – a death too terrible to think about, impossible, unnatural.

Maggie is doing very well. Everyone says so. She's being brave, sensible. She'll be all right, just a little more time maybe . . .

The traffic lights changed to green. I sat up straight and looked in the mirror to check what was behind me. I was doing everything right – everything you're supposed to do when you take your driving test. Check the mirror. Be sure of your stopping distance. Are there pedestrians? Yes, a woman and two children. The road ahead, a thin white line, the other side of the road, a footpath. Hands on the wheel in the ten-to-two position. Everything correct. Strong, sensible hands. A thin white line, third finger, left hand.

Jessica's carrycot was on the back seat. Jessica wasn't in it. Jessica was dead. Ben's old A-to-Z street map was in the pocket of the passenger door. Ben didn't need it. Ben knew where he was going; he'd found the road that he wanted.

Probably not healthy? Carrying your dead baby's carrycot around. An empty carrycot isn't very heavy. Just thirty-three photographs. Married couples often break up after the death of a child. I know that. I'm not stupid. I have a university education. Studied ethics – life and death problems.

There are fifteen of you in a cave far underground, and the only way out is a hole in the roof. A fat man gets stuck in this hole. It's dark. There's not much air left in the cave. You've tried everything to get the fat man through the hole. You have a stick of dynamite.

She'd be six now. Jessica.

Don't shake your head at me, thinking I'm crazy, some kind of madwoman. Look inside your own head – the games and conversations that go on in there. Don't even begin to judge me.

No, I didn't pick up children's dolls and cry over them. No, I didn't want to steal other people's children. I just grieved. For Jessica. I did well. Everyone said so. They were really proud of me.

They became even prouder of me when Ben left. They told me loudly and often how proud they were of me.

I used to play that game, you know? You see a married couple walking in front of you. You imagine the woman gone. You just put your hand in his and go on walking.

I went to the beach one Sunday. There was a dad and his kids. A great father. Our eyes met. I knew I would be a great mother. The children would soon learn to like me . . .

But he didn't come back the next Sunday. Or any Sunday that summer.

Hands on the wheel in the ten-to-two position. Everything correct.
Strong, sensible hands.

I don't hate Ben. But I hate the person that he has changed me into. These lines around my mouth? When your heart starts breaking, you close your teeth, keep your lips tightly shut, keep the screams inside. It shows.

They say I'm still good-looking. Still a wonderful person. Clever too. Should continue my university studies. Studies in ethics. Are humans free to choose their path in life? Who decides what happens to us? Is everything written in the stars?

There's a park near my place. A play-area for children. I noticed this one man came with his little boy every other Sunday. The park, then a pizza, then home to Mummy, until next time. We got to recognize each other, just a look and a smile. Every other Sunday. Unchanging. His family and friends would learn to like me. Love me. Then one weekend he came to our park. With her. They went for a pizza together. Home together. A family. What a bastard.

Freedom to choose is frightening, don't you think? Do you get moments like that? You know, you're driving along, hands on the wheel, everything correct. Then a picture jumps into your head, out of nowhere. Two centimetres. If I move the wheel just two centimetres . . .

Of course, Ben married again. Had twins, two lovely little baby girls. Sometimes I saw them. A family. Together. The walks out with the pushchair. The days out to the zoo.

Then, I saw her on the footpath. Her, with a little hand in each of hers. Me, driving perfectly, doing everything right, not a wrong move.

It was dark, you see. So dark. I couldn't breathe. There was no escape. Just a stick of dynamite in my hands.

Progress

F. SIONIL JOSÉ

🔳

A story from the Philippines, retold by Jennifer Bassett

*Government offices are much the same
everywhere. Sometimes the officials in them
are good people, helpful and kind; sometimes
they are not. And if you need something
badly, sometimes it is necessary to give little
'presents', maybe some money, which then
disappears into a back pocket.*

*These are the ways of the world. People
have been giving and taking bribes for ever.*

Marina Salcedo, Senior Clerk, second grade, hurried to
her desk to open her pay envelope. It was the fifteenth
of July, and tomorrow she was leaving for Manila, to get the
promotion that she had been promised for five years.

She had worked in the Ministry for twenty years, and in
the last five years the cost of living had risen greatly. Without
the extra money from her promotion, her youngest son
would not be able to go to college. Also, three years ago they
had borrowed money on their house when her husband had
had to go to hospital.

She checked her pay carefully. Two hundred and sixty

pesos; this is what she would take to Manila. She walked down to the far end of the hall to the Chief's office. The girls there were not talking. That meant the Chief was in. His secretary told her to go straight in.

The Chief was reading a dirty copy of *Playboy*, a magazine for men full of photos of women. He did not put the magazine away, and Marina stood in front of him, waiting for him to look up. He was about fifty, and going bald.

'So you are leaving tomorrow, Marina,' he said.

'Yes, sir . . .'

'Well, you can have the afternoon off, to get ready. You will only have three working days in Manila. Do you think that will be enough?'

'I would like to have three more days, sir, if possible.'

'No problem, Marina,' the Chief said. 'Oh, and when you are there, will you please buy me the latest gabardine material for a pair of pants? I will pay when you get back.'

'Yes, sir. Thank you.'

Gabardine material – it must cost at least sixty pesos. Last time, the Chief wanted a pair of Levi jeans; they had cost a hundred and twenty pesos. When she returned, they had played this little game: he saying he must pay, she refusing to take the money. After all, he was not a bad boss – three days off with pay, for example. And he did not try to touch her in the way he did with the other women clerks.

🔲

The bus left at six in the morning, driving along the valley through the newly planted rice fields, the water shining in the early morning sun. The roads were good, with strong new bridges, making the journey to Manila only ten hours. It used to take a full day. This was progress, the kind that people could see and enjoy. Marina knew there were problems in the mountain villages and other places, but in her province things were calm. Her own life was not so bad. She and her husband had finally built a house. Three children, one married and soon to leave for the United States; another soon to finish college; and the youngest nearly finished high school. But the cost of living had gone up. They had to cook on wood fires, and could not afford to buy toilet paper.

Five years ago she had asked for promotion. She had gone to Manila twice about it, and finally she had received a notice saying it would happen.

The bus arrived in Manila as it was getting dark. Marina walked to the street where her second cousin lived. They had been college students together. She would probably sleep on a hard sofa in their living room, but that was better than spending thirty pesos on a cheap, dirty room somewhere.

They were having dinner when she arrived and, like a good relation, she had brought meat, fish, and rice from her province. They seemed pleased to see her, but Marina noticed that her cousin soon asked, 'When will you leave?'

'I won't be here more than a week,' she said, 'and I won't eat here. I'll spend every day at the Ministry, following up my papers.'

She was up at six the next day. Her cousin's children, aged thirteen and fourteen, were getting ready for school. They had kept her awake playing rock music in the night.

When she arrived at the Ministry, she went straight to

Personnel. The people that she worked with years ago in that office had all left, and there was nobody she knew. She asked for the person who worked on the papers of staff promotion, and was sent to the other end of the office, to a fat woman in her early thirties, with bad teeth, thin hair, and a uniform that was too small for her large body.

The woman brought out a list and read through it carefully. Then she moved some papers around on her desk, and looked up with a fat little smile.

'I am sorry, Mrs Salcedo, but your name is not here. Maybe the forms got lost . . .'

'But it cannot be,' Marina said. Her voice got louder. 'I have the official letter from you.' She quickly pulled it out of her handbag. 'Here . . . and the file number.'

The woman shook her head, and her fixed little smile did not change.

'Mrs Salcedo,' she said sweetly, 'I will have to look through the files, hundreds and hundreds of them. I will have to ask one of the boys.' She opened the drawer in her desk that was closest to Marina. 'Why don't you drop a twenty-peso bill in here for him . . .?'

For a moment Marina Salcedo could not believe this was happening to her. She worked in the same Ministry as these people. Then she remembered that Anita Botong in her office in the province did the same thing. It had gone on for a long time – too long to be easy to stop. She took a twenty-peso bill from her handbag, and dropped it in the drawer.

'Will I come back this afternoon then?' she asked.

'Oh, Mrs Salcedo,' the woman said, still smiling. 'You

*Marina took a twenty-peso bill from her handbag,
and dropped it in the drawer.*

know how difficult it will be. Why don't you come back early tomorrow?'

'I am from the province . . .'

'Yes, I know. I will do all I can to help you . . .'

She had nothing more to do. She left the Ministry and took a jeepney to the market in Quiapo. What was the best kind of gabardine, she asked, and what did it cost? In the end she bought the material in one of the big department stores for thirty-four pesos. Then she looked round the rest of the market, and found that food prices were higher than at home. So, prices in the province were not so bad then!

She spent five pesos on a bowl of noodles with chicken for lunch, then walked around the city. She had not been to Manila for some time, and it had changed a lot. In Makati, a very rich area, there were tall, glass-sided buildings, and the streets were clean. It was like America. She thought of her son, who would soon be in America. One day in the future she and her husband hoped to join him there. But the future was here, in Makati. And if this was the future, was it necessary to leave the country?

The next morning, back at the Ministry, the fat woman had found her papers, but there was a new form to complete. Marina would have to fetch Form D22a from another office in the building, fill it in, and then take it to Personnel, who would sign it and send it back to the first office. This office was on the fifth floor, and the lift was not working.

The man in the Form D22a office was very sorry. 'Oh,

please come back tomorrow afternoon. We have no forms here at the moment – we have to get some more.'

Marina recognized the old game at once, and was annoyed. The top drawer in the man's desk was open, and Marina dropped a five-peso bill into it. She must remember to carry two-peso bills, she thought.

'Please, I am really in a hurry,' she said. 'Do try and find one. There must be one lying around . . .'

The man closed his desk drawer with a smile, then went to an old filing cabinet behind his desk. It didn't take him a minute to find the form.

The form had a lot of questions, about dates of this and that, school and college, travel abroad . . . That made Marina laugh. How many government clerks have ever traveled abroad? She hadn't even traveled around her own country.

Looking back over her past, she began to think about what she wanted from life. She had never wanted to climb to the top of the tree, to become a minister. Both she and her husband were happy enough with things as they were. After all these years, they had their own home, a piece of land, and they could sleep deeply at night, not worried by the kind of bad dreams that important ministers must have.

She took her completed form to the Chief in the office, who was said to be an honest man. Now was the moment when she would find out if that was true.

She waited and waited, and was at last called over to the glass-topped desk where Chief Bermudez was sitting.

'Well, what is your problem?'

'My promotion, sir,' Marina said. 'I've been waiting a

long time for it.' She put her papers on the desk in front of him.

Chief Bermudez read them all carefully.

'Well, Mrs Salcedo, everything here seems all right. You know what to do next. After I sign the forms, you go to Finance to find out if there are funds to pay you. If there are, the Minister will sign the papers – and you will have your hundred pesos a month. And I think your pay rise should start at the beginning of this year, to give you those extra months. I will make sure that happens.' He began to sign the papers. 'I know you have worked for the Ministry for a long time. Things happen too slowly sometimes – I should not tell you this really – but we must be patient. We must push, and push, and push . . . but only gently.' He smiled. 'Good luck with Finance.'

They were now alone in the room. 'Is that all, sir?' said Marina.

'Why, is there something that I have forgotten?'

In her surprise, Mrs Salcedo forgot to thank him. At the door she decided that Chief Bermudez was a good man. Perhaps she should buy him some gabardine material too. After all, he had added several extra months to her pay rise.

After a quick lunch, just some bananas and a drink, she went to Finance. The girls in the office were sitting talking, or reading newspapers, or doing nothing. The Finance Chief, she was told, was out and would not be in until tomorrow.

Marina left, and decided to go and see a movie.

The next morning she was back in Finance before eight

o'clock. She noticed that the office had several pretty girls, and they seemed to do nothing.

At eight-thirty the Finance Chief arrived, Julio Lobo, one of the top men in the Ministry. He was wearing a brown gabardine suit – she recognized the material at once. She went into his office.

Chief Lobo was reading some files and adding up some figures on a calculator. He looked up at her. There were heavy bags under his eyes, and his thick lips smiled. 'Yes?'

Mrs Salcedo explained her story, telling him she was from the province.

'You can leave your papers here,' he said, still smiling. 'I am in a hurry. I have a meeting in another town today and will not be back until five. You can come and see me then.'

Marina now had to wait all day, and this endless battle to get her promotion was giving her a headache. But it could be worse in other ministries. She knew a teacher who had to pay a thousand pesos just to move to another town.

It was raining outside so she decided to stay in the building and visit the Education office, where she had friends. At three o'clock she went back to wait outside Chief Lobo's office, and tried to read a novel, but it did not hold her interest. The pretty girls in the office were all talking about the disco they were going to that evening.

At five Chief Lobo arrived, and some of the girls went in and out with papers. When they had left, Marina went in.

'Ah, Mrs Salcedo – yes, your papers are still here. I will work on them tomorrow, Saturday. Did you know I work even on Saturday?'

'No, sir.'

'Well, I do.' He smiled, showing teeth yellow from cigarette smoke. He looked at his desk diary, then at her papers again. 'Mmm . . . a hundred pesos a month. Why, that's one thousand two hundred pesos a year. Surely, you can afford to buy me a forty-peso dinner!'

'Yes, of course, sir,' she said.

'Well, then, my favorite Japanese restaurant is in Ermita. It's easy to find. I'll be there on Sunday evening, at seven. I will have your papers – all finished. I see no problem, really.'

'Thank you, sir,' Mrs Salcedo said.

Forty pesos! If she did not eat, she could afford the meal. She would still just have enough to buy her bus ticket.

During Saturday and Sunday morning Marina did not leave her cousin's apartment. Going out meant spending money. So she made rice cakes, cleaned her cousin's kitchen, and washed the floor and the walls in the living room. When the family came home Saturday evening, the place was shining clean, and her cousin was very pleased.

On Sunday afternoon she went out to find the Japanese restaurant. It was mostly foreigners eating there, and it looked very expensive. She would have to give the waiters something too. She must be honest with Chief Lobo, tell him that she did not have the money, that she would give him a present later, when she had got her pay rise.

From there she went to the Manila Hotel, where in 1955 she had danced with her boyfriend, later her husband, when they finished their university studies. It was pleasant to remember those days. But the hotel had changed – it was all

'Sir, you know I am just a poor clerk in the province.
I have only a hundred pesos—'

new inside, with thick carpets and fine wooden furniture. She saw the coffee shop, but she could not afford even one cup of coffee, so she sat on one of the deep soft sofas, watching the beautiful people walking past. So, there was progress under the government's grand new plan, as this fine hotel showed.

At six-thirty she walked back to the Japanese restaurant. Chief Lobo was there, his fat stomach too big for his blue jeans, and his T-shirt smelly from his unwashed body. They sat down, and all around them were the delicious smells of fresh food cooking.

Marina found it hard to speak. 'Sir, you know I am just a poor clerk in the province. I have only a hundred pesos—'

Chief Lobo's hand came down heavily onto her knee, and stayed there. 'My dear woman,' he said. 'We are not going to spend all that. I will just have tea, and . . . some fish. Too much food is bad for me. But making love is not bad for me. So, after this, we go to a motel. That will be no more than forty pesos . . .'

Marina did not want to believe what she had heard. Then she remembered office talk about the Finance Chief – how he behaved towards women, what he asked for . . .

'I have three children, sir,' she said miserably. 'My oldest is married, I have a grandson, the first.'

'That's wonderful,' said Chief Lobo. 'But you know, you don't look like a grandmother.' He looked at her body hungrily, and Marina felt her face turning red. 'You have a good body, very nice . . .'

'Surely, sir, with all those pretty girls in your office . . .'

Chief Lobo laughed. 'Ha! You noticed,' he said. 'But they are young, they need teaching. I don't want to be a teacher all the time. I enjoy beautiful, older women – like you.' His hand moved higher up her leg.

'I am forty-five,' said Marina.

'But you don't look thirty-five!' he said.

She followed him to his car outside in the street. Her mouth was dry with fear. She must be good to him. The future was in his hands. She tried again and again to talk him out of it, but he did not listen.

Alone with him in the motel room at last, she begged him one more time. 'Sir, please. I will give you half the money I get from my promotion. I promise!'

Chief Lobo looked at her in surprise. 'Stupid girl,' he said angrily. 'It's not money I need.' He began to take off his shoes.

When she did not move, he shouted at her. 'Take off your clothes!'

'My poor husband, my poor children,' Marina cried softly as he began to touch her.

▣

She was back at the apartment at nine. She took a long shower, hating Chief Lobo, hating herself, hating the world. How would it be tomorrow when she saw him again? He had not even brought her papers as he had promised.

She did not sleep much that night. When morning came, she knew she must go on, finish the job. After that terrible evening, there was no battle that she could not fight – nothing could stop her now.

Chief Lobo's thick lips smiled at her when she came in.

'We will go up to the Minister's office now,' he said, standing up and picking up her papers.

The Minister's office was very big, with a carpet, paintings on the walls, and tall green plants in the corners.

Minister Guzman was also wearing a brown gabardine suit, but Marina, looking at it closely, realized it was a finer, more expensive material. She had heard that the Minister had a drinking problem. He certainly seemed strange this morning – either sleepy or drunk.

Chief Lobo put Marina's papers on the desk, and the Minister looked through them.

'Ah, Mrs Salcedo . . . your promotion . . . I am very happy to sign these.' To Chief Lobo. 'Are there funds for this?'

'Yes, sir,' Lobo said.

After the Minister had signed the papers, he turned to her again. 'Mrs Salcedo, how is it in your province? What are your problems? It's good to see someone from your province here. You know, your province is very important in our New Society plan.'

Mrs Salcedo looked at him. Was the Minister serious? How could he be so drunk so early in the morning?

She shook her head. 'We have no problems, sir.'

'Come now,' the Minister said. 'Be honest. We need the truth, the facts. Only that way can we make progress.'

Marina shook her head again. 'Everything is fine in our province, sir,' she said.

'All right then,' the Minister said. 'But you must work hard. All of you. You must remember we are building a New Society, progress for the people, a country to be proud of.'

He seemed to be talking to everyone in the office.

'Yes, sir,' Marina said.

'We must all work together. Progress. Promotions are wonderful, but we must work for them. Progress . . .'

After Marina had bought her bus ticket, she had two pesos left. She had made three meat sandwiches at her cousin's, and that would have to be enough until she got home.

When the bus arrived in her town, it was past six and already dark. To save money, she decided to walk home from the bus station. She only had a handbag, a small bag of clothes, the gabardine material, and two apples. Away from the town centre, the road was unlit and rough. She and her family lived on the edge of the town, where they could grow vegetables and keep chickens.

She had just turned a corner when a man jumped out of the shadows and grabbed her handbag. She held on to it as hard as she could, but the man pushed her and she fell, hurting her face on the ground. He took the bag, and as he ran, she shouted after him.

'There's no money in there – just my papers. My papers!'

But he was gone too fast and did not hear her.

She stood up slowly, feeling weak and strange. She still had a long way to walk, and her legs did not want to move. It started to rain, but her umbrella was in the handbag that was stolen. She did not mind the rain; it was losing her papers that felt like a heavy stone lying on her heart. Without the papers, there would be no pay rise. She knew, only too well, that nothing could make Manila send copies of her papers.

A man jumped out of the shadows and grabbed her handbag.
He pushed her and she fell . . .

She would have to return to the capital, and the thought of that filled her heart with fear and misery.

At last she reached her house, with the trees all around it. When she pushed the door open, her family were eating supper and they ran from the table to greet her. They saw the dirt on her clothes, her pale face, her wet untidy hair. To their questions she gave no answers, and Marina Salcedo fell to her knees, the anger and misery coming from her in violent sobbing. No words of kindness, of love, no friendly touch could stop the river of her tears.

The Jacket

GRAEME LAY

A story from New Zealand, retold by Jennifer Bassett

*Young people should be given chances in life
– especially the chance of a good education.
Sometimes that means going to study in
another country, far from home and family.*

*Young Tuaine is at school in New Zealand,
but her home is on a South Sea island, where
the warm waters of the lagoon are as blue as
the sky above . . .*

JUNE 24

I am going to use this big notebook for my diary, and write down everything I feel and do. I brought the book with me when I left home. I used it for English at my school back home, and when I left, there were still plenty of pages not written on, so it will be good for a diary. At home I read a story called *The Diary of Anne Frank*. It was a very sad story, but I read it lots of times. Anne said it made her feel better to write things down, it helped her with all those troubles she had, so maybe my diary will help me feel better too.

Tomorrow it will be two months since I left home to come here. 61 days. Just two numbers when I write it like that, 61 days, but it is the slowest and longest time I can remember. How can 61 days go so slowly? I still think of home all the time, and I can remember every little thing about the island, except how warm it was. I can't remember that, because here it is so cold all the time, but when I lie here and close my eyes I can see my friends, and my family, and all my favourite places. Mama and Papa, and Mele and Metua, and Rima, and the big black rock where we swam in the lagoon, and the path that goes to the top of our mountain, and the cool wind at the top. And if sometimes I can't remember everything, there are the photos by my bed, and all my seashells.

When I was a baby, I was given to my grandparents, because I was the youngest in our family, and that is our custom. My real parents live on another island. Our village is called Vaipaka, and our house is a little bit back from the road that goes through the village, by the hill. When the last big storm – called Sharon – came, the waves from the lagoon came right over the road, but not as far as our garden, which was lucky. The wind blew all the flowers out of our garden, but at least the roof stayed on our house, not like at Mele's place. A great piece of metal blew off their roof, right over the house, and cut their goat's head off. It was terrible for the poor animal. There were some bad things that happened in our village, like Sharon, and some accidents on the motorbikes, but mostly there were good things, and I remember the good things, not the bad things.

School was good too, I liked it at the college, and I nearly always came top of my class. But I'm sorry about that now, it was coming top that probably sent me away. We had exams in the first term, and I came first or second in every exam. Mr Ashton, the teacher, came to our house and said to Mama and Papa that our school on the island wasn't good enough for me, that I should go to school in New Zealand. Mama and Papa talked about it to Uncle George. I was worried, because I didn't want to go away, but they talked about it again with Mr Ashton, and all my family put in some money for the plane and sent me here to Aunty Vaine's.

Aunty Vaine is my mother's cousin, and she has been living in Auckland for over twenty years. There's four of us here in her house: Aunty, Ta (he's seventeen), Marlene, and me. Marlene and I sleep in the same bedroom. She's six. The week after I arrived, Aunty bought me a uniform, and I started at the girls' college. I've got to stop my diary now, the video has finished, and Marlene wants to go to bed.

JUNE 25

At first, Aunty was friendly. She asked me all about home and all the relations she hadn't seen for so long, and she told me the things she used to do when she was a girl on the island. Then she asked me how much money did I bring with me from the island, and I said I didn't bring any, and she got a bit angry. I told her Mama and Papa didn't have any money to give me, and they told me that Aunty had a good job and earned plenty of money. Aunty said she worked in the chicken factory, but she didn't get much money and most of it went on paying the rent for the house. Then I asked her where was my uncle? I didn't like to ask about him at first because perhaps he had left her or something. Aunty started crying then and told me about the accident. Uncle Ben worked for a building company that made bridges. One day one of those very long, heavy pieces of metal fell on him. His back was broken, and he died in hospital. I told her I was very sorry I didn't know about the accident, nobody at home heard about it. She said Uncle Ben didn't come from our islands, he was from Niue, so she only told his family. I felt really sad for Aunty then, and bad that I came to live with her when she didn't have enough money.

JULY 1

I haven't been able to write in my diary recently. I have had too much schoolwork to do. School is very hard here, but the teachers are nice. My class teacher Mrs Price is best, she's great, she introduced me to lots of girls. But they aren't from my island, they're Samoans, and their language is very strange to me. The school is so big, too, over a thousand girls, and so many rooms. It is scary, in a school where there are so many strangers. Everyone seems cleverer than me, their English is so good. I try hard to keep up, but I get much lower marks than I did at home. I don't have enough time to do my work, that's the trouble. Aunty is working evenings at the chicken factory, and I have to get the dinner every night. The only place I can study is in the bedroom, and the noise from the video is so bad. Every night Ta gets some videos, and always they are noisy, full of shooting and wars and shouting. I hate that Sylvester Stallone. I think it's

It is scary, in a school where there are so many strangers.
Everyone seems cleverer than me . . .

bad for Ta to watch just that kind of video. Marlene too. Yesterday I went and asked Ta please could he turn the video down because I was trying to study in my room, and he got angry and shouted bad words at me. He thinks he's so special. What a laugh, he's just a stupid boy who can't get a job. He won't turn down the video. I'm going to bed now.

JULY 5

It's Sunday, but we didn't go to church. Aunty used to go to church but she never goes now. When I asked why, she said she didn't believe in God any more. I thought that was terrible and I asked her why. She said it was because God took Uncle Ben away from them, and left them with no one to take care of them, and not enough money. I don't know if that's right, but I can understand the way Aunty feels. I'm not sure about God. He can be very cruel sometimes, even to good people like Anne Frank and Uncle Ben.

In the afternoon we took the bus to visit Uncle Ben's grave. There is a smiling photo on the grey stone, and shiny black letters. BENJAMIN FILIGI, AGED 48 YEARS, MUCH LOVED HUSBAND AND FATHER. We all cried at the grave, even Ta, when Aunty put the flowers on it. In the photo on his grave, Uncle Ben looks like he was a nice man.

JULY 10

I didn't go to school today. I wanted to, but it's a long way and I have to get the bus, and the bus ticket costs a lot of money. Aunty said she didn't have any money left. She was getting angry with me, so I thought I will walk to school tomorrow instead of getting the bus. Today I tried to do my schoolwork by myself at home, but I didn't do very well.

July 11

I am very tired tonight. This morning I got up at six o'clock and made some sandwiches for my lunch, and I left before any of the others were up. It was still dark, and very scary because there was nobody in the streets. I walked right down Dominion Road, and slowly the sky got lighter. My school bag was hurting my shoulder, and I was trying to remember the way the bus went from the time when I had a ticket. In the end I got to the school, but it took a long long time and I was late, and the teacher at the gate took my name and I had a detention. That was the first time I ever had one. My class teacher Mrs Price asked me why I was late. I didn't like to tell her my Aunty didn't have any money for the bus, so I said I slept in. Mrs Price asked me how I was getting on here, and she seemed a bit worried. At lunchtime she brought a fifth-form girl called Moana who was from my country to see me. Moana and I talked in our language. She doesn't come from my island, but I knew some cousins of hers. I enjoyed talking to Moana, but it made me sad because I began thinking about home and all the people I knew.

When I told Moana about walking to school, she took me to the school library and showed me a street map. We saw that there was a much shorter way for me to come to school, I don't have to follow the bus route. Moana asked me if I would like to come to her place one day, but I saw on the map that she lives at Te Atatu, too far away from my place.

I walked home that quicker way that I found on the map, but because of my detention I didn't get home until six o'clock. I am very tired tonight, I can't write any more.

JULY 12

Aunty gave me two dollars this morning. I had to decide if I will spend it on the bus fare or some lunch. There was only fried bananas for breakfast because Aunty doesn't get paid until tomorrow, so I decided to walk to school and buy my lunch. At the end of one street there was a bridge over the motorway that was just for pedestrians. I stopped and looked down at the motorway. All those cars! It was like a great river running into the city. Then it started to rain. It rained and rained, very heavy, like it does at home, but very cold. I don't have a coat or jacket, so I got wet through, on my hair, down my neck, on my legs, in my shoes. I kept on walking towards school, and getting wetter and wetter and colder and colder. Then I saw a clock on a building that said five minutes to nine. That was too late for school so I turned round and walked home again, and I was so cold I had to get into bed to keep warm. I didn't get up until Marlene came home from school.

JULY 13

Aunty is working daytime at the factory now, so she told Marlene and me to stay home from school and do the shopping. We walked to the supermarket and after we had done the shopping there was some money left over. We were very hungry, so I got us some Kentucky Fried Chicken for lunch. It was so good! Marlene and I took the chicken to the park and ate it there. When people went past us, they stared. I knew they were thinking, why aren't those girls at school? Maybe they would tell the police, so I said to Marlene come on, we ought to get home now. I felt bad about using Aunty's money for Kentucky Fried Chicken, and I told Marlene not to say we had it. I won't do that again. I went to bed in the afternoon, I didn't feel very well. My head aches and I think I'm getting a cold.

JULY 18

I didn't write in my diary for a few days, because I stayed in bed with a really bad cold. I felt miserable. I've missed a lot of school now, and I don't know how I will catch up. Exams are next month and I'm very worried about them. Always at home I did well in exams, but I can't here. I lie on my bed and stare at my photos and the trochus shell that Papa gave me. When I put the shell to my ear, I can hear the lagoon whispering to me. The trochus shells are very special to us. Once every year the people from the villages can get the trochus from the lagoon, but only a few for each family, so there will always be more for next year. The shells are polished for the tourists. But Papa polished this trochus just for me, and it is so beautiful with all the different colours, it is like holding a rainbow in my hand. Even the darkness here doesn't stop the trochus from shining.

JULY 19

I had a very bad day today. When I woke up, I decided I must go to school and catch up my work so I will do well in exams

'I haven't even got enough money for my own children!'
Aunty shouted. 'Why did you have to come here anyway?'

and get a good report to send home to Mama and Papa. So I said to Aunty I'm going back to school, I'm walking but please could I have some money for my lunch? Then Aunty got very mad, and she shouted at me: 'I've got no money left for you! I haven't even got enough money for my own children! Why did you have to come here anyway?'

I told her I didn't really want to come, and I'm sorry for all this trouble I am giving her. I said I don't like it here and I want to go home. Aunty got even angrier and said she didn't even have enough money for the bus, so how is she going to pay for a plane ticket? She said she didn't ask me to come here, she only said yes because she couldn't say no to her family. She said if I want to go home my family should send the money to pay, and I said they couldn't because they spent all their money sending me here. I felt really miserable then and ran out of the room, crying.

Everything here is money. Money for food, money for buses, money for warm clothes, money for shoes. Back home we only need money for the motorbike and a bit of food from the shop. We get everything from the lagoon and the fields, and we don't worry about money. But here money makes me frightened, because there isn't enough, and I feel bad that Aunty has to get more because of me. I don't know what to do. There is no telephone here to ring, or at home. All I can do is lie on my bed and stare at my photos and hold my trochus shell. No school again today.

July 20
Raining again. I didn't go to school. I did some cleaning in

the house and watched some TV. There was a knock on the door but I didn't answer it. The person put a letter in the letter box, and later I went out to get it. It was addressed to Aunty, and I opened it. It said because I hadn't been to school, my Aunty should visit the school immediately. I put the letter in the rubbish. I don't want Aunty to get mad again, but I'm worried. I know it's against the law to not go to school but I can't go back. I'm too far behind. Perhaps I can leave school and get a job in an office. That would help Aunty with the money.

JULY 21

So much happened today, I never had a day like it in my life. Ta gave me some money for the bus, and told me how to get downtown. I caught the bus and ended up in Queen Street, the first time I have been there. So many grand buildings! It was like a TV programme. I began to walk up Queen Street, but there was a freezing cold wind, and then it started to rain, and felt even colder. I couldn't stop staring in the shop windows. All those lovely things! In one shop they were selling holidays, and there was a big photograph of home, showing my island! It was a very beautiful picture, the lagoon so blue, and the sea all around so dark, and the whiteness where the waves break on the reef round the lagoon. I wanted to say to people in the street, 'Look, there's my island, isn't it beautiful?' But all the people were just hurrying past, not stopping, not noticing.

I kept on walking up Queen Street, I was looking for a clothes shop, because I needed a jacket. The wind went right through my clothes, I felt I wasn't wearing anything at all. I came to a very big shop and went in. There were lots and lots of jackets, but I saw one of the shop people staring at me, so I went back out into the cold and kept on walking. After a while I came to another shop which sold jackets. I was very worried about what I was going to do, but I was so cold and I didn't really care how wrong it was. I just didn't want to get caught. I went into the shop and started looking at the jackets. I had a white supermarket bag in my pocket, and I got it out, took a blue jacket and put it in the bag as quickly as I could. My hands were shaking, and I wanted to run, but instead I walked around slowly and pretended to look at some coats, then I walked out. I didn't stop until I got to the bridge over the motorway. I took out the jacket and saw the price on it – 125 dollars! I put it on. It was so warm! It's got wool inside and it keeps the rain out and everything. I wore it to just before I got home. Then I put it back in the bag and hid it under my bed.

JULY 22

I couldn't sleep all last night. It was very bad to take that jacket from the shop. The church says you must not steal, and I can't forget that. I have heard it all my life. I won't wear the jacket again. I am too ashamed. Anne Frank did not steal, not even food when she was nearly dead from hunger.

JULY 23

Saturday today. Ta got three videos, all fighting and shooting. I can hear through the wall, and it sounds like a war is going

*We used to go across to the little island of Tokoa, and sit
under the trees and have fruit drinks. It was beautiful there . . .*

on. At home on Saturday night we used to go across to the big holiday hotel on the little island of Tokoa. We used to sit under the trees and have fruit drinks, and watch the dancing for the tourists. It was beautiful there, and I loved the dancing and the music. I want to dance at Tokoa when I am older. I decided what to do about the jacket. On Monday I will take it back to the shop.

JULY 25

So much happened today. I will have to write it down very carefully to make sure I don't miss anything. When I woke up I put the jacket in my school bag and told my Aunty I'm going to school. I walked into town and waited until it was after nine o'clock, then I walked to the shop. There weren't many people inside, and I went over to where the jackets were and quickly started to take the jacket out of my bag. But as I did it, I looked up and saw a lady with grey hair watching me from the other side of some dresses. She saw what I was doing and came over.

'What are you doing? Did you take this?' she said. Her voice was very cross. I couldn't explain to her that I was bringing it back because I had taken it before. I thought she wouldn't believe me. She said, 'Come with me,' and she took my arm and we went over to the back of the shop. I started to cry.

We went into an office, and there was a man in there sitting at a desk. He was a young man in a suit. The lady told him she had found me taking the jacket, and the man said, 'Is this right?' and I just nodded. I couldn't stop crying, so I couldn't explain. I will have to go to court, I thought, and my family will be so ashamed of me.

The man told me to sit down and he rang someone on his telephone. 'It's a shoplifter,' he said. Then the man asked me my name and my address and my school, and I told him those things.

After a bit a police lady came in, and the shop lady went out. The police lady was young and pretty, with dark hair. She sat down and asked me questions in a kind voice, and it was easier to talk to her than those other ones. I told her all about the jacket and what I did.

She said to the man, 'I think she's telling the truth, and I think we should talk to someone from the school first.'

The man looked cross, but he said, 'All right, I have to agree. This is unusual.'

'Very unusual,' the police lady said. 'I never heard of a shoplifter who took back what she stole.' She smiled at me, and asked, 'Who would you like us to talk to from school?'

When Mrs Price came in, she looked just as usual, not worried or anything. But I started crying again because I was so ashamed, and she sat down next to me and said, 'Don't worry, Tuaine, everything will be all right.'

Then she and the police lady talked, and they seemed really friendly to each other. I don't think the shop manager liked that and he still looked angry. Mrs Price asked me why I hadn't been to school. She has got grey hair, but her face is young and she talks in a very kind way. I told her about the money, and Aunty and my uncle and how he was killed. And about the exams and how I was worried about them, and how I got cold when I went out and how I took the jacket. I said I was very ashamed for what I did.

When my story was finished, Mrs Price looked at the police lady, and then they both looked at the manager. The police lady said, 'The jacket has been returned, Mr Jackson, and I really don't think this girl is a thief.' The manager didn't look at her, but he nodded his head.

I said to him, 'I'm very sorry I took your jacket. I will never do it again.' He stood up and nodded again, and Mrs Price said, 'I'll take you home now, Tuaine.'

Mrs Price and I sat in her car outside my house. She talked slowly and I felt she was thinking deeply about everything she was saying.

She said, 'We can give you extra lessons at school to help you catch up. And I'll find out if your Aunty can get some money from the government, I'm sure she can. That will help with the clothes problem . . .'

Then Mrs Price stopped, and she looked at me for a long time without speaking. She has very clear grey eyes, very kind and understanding, and her eyes seemed to see a long way into me.

'Or,' she said in a slow voice, 'would you just like us to arrange for you to go home?'

I looked back into those grey, kind eyes. The way she said it, I knew it was really possible. Tears came back into my eyes. Through them I saw a house, and faces, and the lagoon, shining and blue.

'I would like to go home,' I said.

My Little Ghost

DAVID A. KULU

A story from Papua New Guinea, retold by Jennifer Bassett

Very young children like to feel safe. They like the same things to happen every day; they like the same people around them. They like what they know, and are often afraid of what they don't know.

Avusi is worried. Why does his mama work in a house full of ghosts – white ghosts?

I live in a small village on the coast in Papua New Guinea. My name is Avusi. My Mama, she works in town, looking after somebody's children. Every morning I wake up to the sound of my Mama getting ready for work, and I am filled with a feeling of sadness.

'Mama, can I come with you?'

'No, my brave little man, you cannot come.'

'But I don't want to stay here by myself,' I cry.

'Your Bubu will be here to look after you, and you have all the other children in the village to play with.'

I watch unhappily as my mother goes down the wooden steps of our hut and disappears into the morning fog.

That night, while my mother was putting me to bed, I asked her about her job.

'Mama, is it true there are lots of ghosts where you work?'

'Why? Who told you a story like that?' she asked.

'Bubu Man said you work in a house full of white ghosts.'

'Don't listen to that old man. One day he'll frighten you to death. I don't work in a house of white ghosts, is that clear?'

'Yes, Mama.'

'So, I guess that means you're not coming with me to work tomorrow . . . because *you* think I work in a house full of ghosts.'

'No, I want to come, I want to come, please!' I said.

'OK, OK, you can come,' she laughed.

Next day I got up at the same time as the sun.

'Mama, Mama, wake up!' I called, running into my mother's room. 'You're going to be late for work.'

'If you're not ready soon, I'll have to leave you,' said my Mama.

I turned round to find her all dressed and ready. I ran out of the room realizing that I had woken up late.

We climbed into a PMV and drove away into town. This was only the second time I had been in a PMV. We got off in front of a big white house. Inside the gate there was green grass and beautiful flowers of so many colours – it was like walking through a rainbow. I asked my mother the question that had been in my head all the way there.

'You said that there are no ghosts?'

'No ghosts,' she said. 'Sure as the day you were born.'

As the door opened, my mouth fell open too. In front of me was the biggest room I had ever seen. It was a palace.

*So I put my arms round the little white ghost,
who was called Brandon.*

'Maria, Maria!' It was the voices of children. Running towards us were two little white ghosts. I held on to my mother's dress, shaking with fright. But my mother picked up the little white ghosts and held them in her arms. Then around the corner came a larger white ghost, the same size as my mother, but with long golden hair and carrying a little white baby ghost.

'Good morning, Maria,' the big ghost said. 'And you must be Avusi.'

She put out her hand to touch me, but I moved away.

'Don't be afraid, honey, it's OK,' said my mother. 'They're not ghosts.'

'Ghosts?' laughed the big ghost. 'Here,' she said, putting the baby down on the floor.

The baby made a baby kind of noise and smiled, then came towards me and grabbed me round the waist. I shut my eyes, hoping and hoping that the ghosts would go away. But after a while I realized that this baby ghost felt like me. I opened my eyes just a little bit, and looked down.

'He's smiling at me . . . he likes me.'

'Yes, he does,' smiled the big white ghost.

So I put my arms round the little white ghost, who was called Brandon. There and then I learnt that not everyone had the same skin colour as me. I knew I had made a friend, and it didn't matter what crazy story my grandfather had told me – this ghost was my friend. He was my little ghost.

GLOSSARY

aid *(n)* money, food, etc. that is sent to help other countries

bastard *(taboo, slang)* a very rude word for somebody, usually a man, who has been unpleasant or cruel

beggar *(n)* someone who lives by asking people for money

bubu *(Papua New Guinea English)* grandparent

carrycot a small bed for a baby, which can be carried

chairman the person who is the head of a committee

clerk someone who does paperwork in an office

committee a group of people who make decisions in a project

court the place where law trials take place and crimes are judged

culture the customs, belief, art, way of life, etc. of a country

custom the way a person always does something

department one of the parts of a government, big company, etc.

detention having to stay later at school as a punishment

development (of a country) becoming more modern, richer, more successful

diplomat a person whose job is to speak for their country in a foreign country

doll a child's toy in the shape of a person

dynamite something that explodes, like a small bomb

ethics moral principles or rules of behaviour

expert a person who is especially good at something

file *(n)* a box or piece of card for keeping loose papers together

filing cabinet a piece of office furniture where files are kept

finance money used to run a project, a part of government, etc.;
Finance the department where finance people work

form *(n)* a piece of paper with questions and spaces for answers

funds money that is available to be spent

gabardine a strong material used for making coats, trousers, etc.

government the group of people who control a country

grab to take something with your hand suddenly or roughly

grave a place in the ground where a dead person is buried

grieve to feel very sad, especially when somebody has died

hut a small, very simply built house, usually one or two rooms

jacket a short coat

jeepney *(Philippine English)* a kind of taxi, originally made from US military jeeps from World War II; they are colourful, crowded, and a symbol of Philippine culture

lagoon a lake of salt water that is separated from the sea by a reef

look after to take care of something or somebody

minister a senior member of the government who is in charge of a government department

ministry a government department that has a special area of work, for example, education

newsletter a printed report containing news of an organization

nod *(v)* to move your head up and down to show agreement

official *(n)* an important person in an organization

oral spoken, not written

organization a group of people who work together for a special purpose (e.g. the United Nations is a very big organization)

pants *(American English)* trousers

pedestrian a person walking in the street (not travelling in a car)

personnel the people who work for an organization; **Personnel** the department which deals with employment, training, etc.

PMV *(Papua New Guinea English)* Public Motor Vehicle, a kind of unofficial bus

polish *(v)* to make something smooth and shiny by rubbing it

progress improving, developing, moving towards a goal

project a big plan to do something

promotion moving to a more important job, with more money

province an area of a country, usually away from the capital city

publish to prepare and print a book, newsletter, magazine, etc.

pushchair a seat on wheels in which a child is pushed along

rainbow a half circle of different colours in the sky when the sun shines through rain

reef a long line of rocks near the surface of the sea

relation a person in your family

rule something that tells you what you must or must not do

scary *(informal)* frightening

seashell the empty shell of a small animal that lives in the sea

self-respect feeling proud of yourself because what you do, say, etc. is right and good

senior higher in rank or status than other people

shit *(taboo, slang)* a swear word, used to show that you are angry; it also means the solid waste matter that comes out of your body

shoplifter somebody who steals from shops

sob *(v & n)* to cry loudly, making short sounds

soul the part of a person that some people believe does not die when the body dies

tradition something that people in a certain place have done or believed for a long time

trochus shell a kind of seashell found on reefs in the Pacific

twin one of two people who were born at the same time from the same mother

VIP (Very Important Person) a famous or important person

ACTIVITIES

Before Reading

Before you read the stories, read the introductions at the beginning, then use these activities to help you think about the stories. How much can you guess or predict?

1 *The Glorious Pacific Way* (story introduction page 1). Do you agree (A) or disagree (D) with these ideas?

   1 It is very important to write down oral traditions before they are lost for ever.

   2 Young people in every culture like to hear the stories that their grandparents tell them.

   3 The world has changed a lot in the last hundred years. Old stories may be interesting, but they don't have much meaning or importance for the modern world.

   4 The government should give Ole a typewriter to help him.

2 *Maggie* (story introduction page 16). What can you guess about the woman in this story? Choose some of these ideas.

   1 Maggie's child has died recently.

   2 Maggie has put her child's death behind her, and is getting on with her life.

   3 Maggie's friends are saying hopeful things about Maggie, but in fact they are very worried about her.

   4 Maggie's friends think she'll be all right very soon.

   5 Maggie's unhappiness is very, very great.

3 *Progress* (story introduction page 20). What do you think about bribes? Choose words to complete this passage which express your ideas best.

In *(all / most / some)* countries of the world, people give and take bribes. It happens in *(governments / schools)* and in *(families / businesses)*. Small bribes are often *(food / cash)* in the hand, but big bribes can be *(millions / hundreds)* of dollars in a personal bank account. It is a *(wrong / very bad)* thing to do, *(and / but)* it is *(sometimes / never)* necessary to give a bribe.

4 *The Jacket* (story introduction page 37). What can you guess about this story? Choose one or more of these ideas.

1 Tuaine is a clever student.
2 Tuaine is very homesick for her island.
3 Tuaine makes a lot of new friends in New Zealand.
4 The cold, wet weather in New Zealand is hard for Tuaine.
5 Tuaine gets into trouble.
6 Tuaine learns to like New Zealand and does well at school.
7 Tuaine goes home to her island and stays there.

5 *My Little Ghost* (story introduction page 54). What will happen to Avusi? Choose endings for these sentences.

1 In this story Avusi will meet . . .
   a) a ghost.   b) an old man.   c) a baby.
2 At the end of the story Avusi will be . . .
   a) afraid.   b) happy.   c) dead.

ACTIVITIES

After Reading

1 **Here are the thoughts of five characters (one from each story). Which characters are they, and from which story? Who or what are they thinking about?**

1 'I feel sorry for her, of course I do. But it was my child too. She never seems to remember that. But you can't grieve for ever. It's hard, but you have to put it behind you, move on, start again . . .'

2 'This is my home, and she's just a kind of cousin. But she thinks she can tell me what to do! *Ooh, I can't study with all those noisy videos playing.* Well, too bad. She'll have to learn to live with my videos . . .'

3 'Well, how was I supposed to know they were important? They just looked like old school notebooks. Why would anyone want to keep those? I thought I'd found a really good use for all that paper . . .'

4 'Oh good, she's brought him with her today. He does look frightened, hiding behind her skirt like that. It's all very new to him. Maybe he'd like to play with the baby . . .'

5 'Here's one of these clerks from the provinces. You can always recognize them. I expect she wants her promotion papers. I think I'll ask for ten – no, twenty. I'll say it's for one of the boys . . .'

2 Here is Emi Bagarap, in *The Glorious Pacific Way*, talking to Ole's other friend, Manu. Use these words to complete the passage (one word for each gap).

cabinets, committee, development, filing, funds, honest, newsletter, rich, rules, selling, sensible, simple, traditions, typewriter

'No, no, the trouble with Ole is that he's too _____. He said he just wanted a _____ and some _____ _____, to help him in his project about oral _____. But _____ money is not easy to get. You have to find a group of people and start a _____, write letters, publish a _____, things like that. And then the _____ will start to come in. No, he's not _____ his soul! He's just learnt to be _____. The _____ countries have the money, and they make the _____. It's as _____ as that.'

3 In *Progress*, Marina tells her Chief that her handbag was stolen. Here are two replies from him. Which reply do you think fits the story best? Which reply do you like best, and why?

1 'I'm very sorry to hear about your troubles, Marina. That's a terrible thing to happen. Now, this is what I'll do. I'll write to Manila for you today, and tell them to send copies of your promotion papers at once. You must have your pay rise; you've earned it. So don't worry.'

2 'Of course I'm very sorry about the robbery. That's bad luck. But no promotion papers, no pay rise – you know the rules. And I won't allow you more time off to go back to Manila. You'll have to live without your pay rise, that's all.'

4 **At the end of the story *Maggie* we don't really know what is going to happen. What do *you* think happens next? Choose one of these ideas and complete it in your own words.**

1 Maggie turned the wheel, and the car went off the road, up onto the footpath, and _____.

2 Maggie drove straight on past, with tears running down her face. She _____.

3 At that moment Maggie stopped the car. She got out, telephoned her doctor, and asked _____.

5 **When Tuaine got home, perhaps her friend Mele asked what had happened. Put their conversation in the right order, and write in the speakers' names. Mele speaks first (number 3).**

1 _____ 'Oh, I see. That's awful. Did they catch you?'

2 _____ 'Well, I – I stole a jacket from a shop.'

3 _____ 'Hi, Tuaine. What are you doing here?'

4 _____ 'Yes, but the police lady was nice. She called Mrs Price, my teacher at school, and she came and – and—'

5 _____ 'Oh, Tuaine, that's terrible! Why did you do that?'

6 _____ 'I've come home. I got into trouble, you see.'

7 _____ 'Oh, don't cry, Tuaine! Everything's all right now.'

8 _____ 'Because I was so cold. I didn't have a coat and I couldn't buy one. My aunty didn't have any money.'

9 _____ 'The police! But you were taking it back . . .!'

10 _____ 'No, they didn't. But I tried to take it back to the shop later, and they caught me and called the police.'

11 _____ 'Trouble? What kind of trouble?'

6 **What did you think about these stories? Complete these sentences in your own words.**

1 The saddest story was _____ because . . .

2 The funniest story was _____ because . . .

3 The story _____ made me angry because . . .

4 The most frightening story was _____ because . . .

5 The nicest story was _____ because . . .

7 **Here is a short poem (a kind of poem called a haiku) about one of the stories. Which of the five stories is it about?**

> *First, the long journey;*
> *then, greedy clerks; and now this.*
> *A hard promotion.*

Here is another haiku, about the same story.

> *Six days she waited,*
> *filled in forms, paid every bribe,*
> *and all for nothing.*

A haiku is a Japanese poem, which is always in three lines, and the three lines always have 5, 7, and 5 syllables each, like this:

| First | the | long | jour | ney | = 5 syllables

| then | greed | y | clerks | and | now | this | = 7 syllables

| A | hard | pro | mo | tion | = 5 syllables

Now write your own haiku, one for each of the other four stories. Think about what each story is really about. What are the important ideas for you? Remember to keep to three lines of 5, 7, 5 syllables each.

ABOUT THE AUTHORS

EPELI HAU'OFA

Epeli Hau'ofa (1939–2009) was born in Papua New Guinea of Tongan parents, and was educated in Papua, Tonga, Fiji, Australia, and Canada. He was a Professor of Sociology and of Anthropology, and worked for the King of Tonga as Keeper of Palace Records. In 1997 he founded the Oceania Centre for Arts and Culture. His books include a novel, short stories, and several academic studies and reports. His story *The Glorious Pacific Way* comes from *Tales of the Tikongs* (1983), a collection of stories about Tiko (an imaginary island very like Tonga). He spent his last years in Fiji on a small farm, where he planted tropical trees that will be fully grown after 300 years, and Chinese cabbage that is ready to eat after three weeks.

DENISE WHITTAKER

Denise Whittaker is an experienced writer and teacher of creative writing. She was born in Gibraltar, where her father was with the Royal Air Force. She lived in many countries, and continues to live a wandering life. Her work includes short plays and an award-winning short film, and she has published stories, poems, articles, and book reviews. She is now working on a novel. Her story *Maggie* was the Australia and New Zealand winner of the Commonwealth Short Story competition 2003–4. Denise says that her story-telling skills come from her mother, aunts, and sisters, the story-keepers who remember and retell all the family events and traditions.

F. SIONIL JOSÉ

Francisco Sionil José (1924–) was born in the Philippines, and spent his childhood in Barrio Cabugawan, Rosales. His love of books and reading began early at school, and later, while working as a journalist in Manila, he started writing short stories and novels. He wrote in English rather than in his native language Ilokano, or his national language Tagalog. His first novel was published in 1962, and since then he has published twelve novels, seven books of short stories, poetry, and books of essays. He is one of the most widely read Filipino writers in the English language, and has received many awards. In 2001 he was given the order of National Artist of the Phillipines for Literature.

   As a child, José knew what it was like to be poor and hungry, and in his novels and short stories he writes with feeling and passion about the lives of Filipino families. His most famous work is the *Rosales Saga*, a series of five novels which covers three centuries of Philippine history and social change. In a lecture given in 2007 he said, 'You ask me why I write . . . What writers do is create the cultural foundation of a nation. I want to relive our history. I want to give our people memory. My tradition is the village. My tradition is this small town. In many ways, I never really left Barrio Cabugawan.'

DAVID A. KULU

David Avusi Kulu (1978–) was born in Canberra, Australia, the youngest son of Papua New Guinean parents. His father was a diplomat, and David spent most of his childhood in Jakarta, Indonesia. His story *My Little Ghost*, one of the winning stories in the Commonwealth Short Story competition 2003–4, is based on his time as a child in Jakarta, where people thought he was 'different' because of his 'afro' hair. After studying law at the

University of Papua New Guinea, he now works as a lawyer in a big company, and continues to write stories, to share them with his young daughter. He hopes his daughter will appreciate the stories of childhood because, he says, 'They are with you for a lifetime. I, for one, can still remember the first story that was read to me. Maybe one day she'll be able to read my stories to her children, and even her grandchildren.'

GRAEME LAY

Graeme Lay (1944–) was born in Foxton, New Zealand, and grew up in Taranaki. After graduating from Victoria University of Wellington, he taught in New Zealand and England. Since 1997 he has been a full-time writer, working from his home on Auckland's North Shore. He writes short stories, novels for adults and young adults, non-fiction and travel stories. Much of his fiction and non-fiction is set in the islands of the South Pacific, a region in which he has travelled widely. His latest book is *In Search of Paradise – Artists and Writers in the colonial South Pacific* (2008).

His story *The Jacket* was first published in *Metro* magazine, and was the co-winner of the John Cowie Reid Award for Short Fiction in 1989. This story later evolved into a novel for young adults, *Leaving One Foot Island* (1998), which was a finalist in the 1999 New Zealand Post Children's Book Awards. However, young Tuaine Takamoa's story did not end there. She returned to her home island – beautiful Aitutaki in the Cook Islands – and Graeme Lay continued the story of her life and loves in two further young adult novels, *Return to One Foot Island* (2002), which was also a finalist in the New Zealand Post Children's Book Awards, and *The Pearl of One Foot Island* (2004).

OXFORD BOOKWORMS LIBRARY

Classics • Crime & Mystery • Factfiles • Fantasy & Horror
Human Interest • Playscripts • Thriller & Adventure
True Stories • World Stories

The OXFORD BOOKWORMS LIBRARY provides enjoyable reading in English, with a wide range of classic and modern fiction, non-fiction, and plays. It includes original and adapted texts in seven carefully graded language stages, which take learners from beginner to advanced level. An overview is given on the next pages.

All Stage 1 titles are available as audio recordings, as well as over eighty other titles from Starter to Stage 6. All Starters and many titles at Stages 1 to 4 are specially recommended for younger learners. Every Bookworm is illustrated, and Starters and Factfiles have full-colour illustrations.

The OXFORD BOOKWORMS LIBRARY also offers extensive support. Each book contains an introduction to the story, notes about the author, a glossary, and activities. Additional resources include tests and worksheets, and answers for these and for the activities in the books. There is advice on running a class library, using audio recordings, and the many ways of using Oxford Bookworms in reading programmes. Resource materials are available on the website <www.oup.com/bookworms>.

The *Oxford Bookworms Collection* is a series for advanced learners. It consists of volumes of short stories by well-known authors, both classic and modern. Texts are not abridged or adapted in any way, but carefully selected to be accessible to the advanced student.

You can find details and a full list of titles in the *Oxford Bookworms Library Catalogue* and *Oxford English Language Teaching Catalogues*, and on the website <www.oup.com/bookworms>.

THE OXFORD BOOKWORMS LIBRARY
GRADING AND SAMPLE EXTRACTS

STARTER • 250 HEADWORDS

present simple – present continuous – imperative –
can/cannot, must – *going to* (future) – simple gerunds …

Her phone is ringing – but where is it?

Sally gets out of bed and looks in her bag. No phone. She looks under the bed. No phone. Then she looks behind the door. There is her phone. Sally picks up her phone and answers it. *Sally's Phone*

STAGE 1 • 400 HEADWORDS

… past simple – coordination with *and*, *but*, *or* –
subordination with *before, after, when, because, so* …

I knew him in Persia. He was a famous builder and I worked with him there. For a time I was his friend, but not for long. When he came to Paris, I came after him – I wanted to watch him. He was a very clever, very dangerous man. *The Phantom of the Opera*

STAGE 2 • 700 HEADWORDS

… present perfect – *will* (future) – *(don't) have to, must not, could* –
comparison of adjectives – simple *if* clauses – past continuous –
tag questions – *ask/tell* + infinitive …

While I was writing these words in my diary, I decided what to do. I must try to escape. I shall try to get down the wall outside. The window is high above the ground, but I have to try. I shall take some of the gold with me – if I escape, perhaps it will be helpful later. *Dracula*

STAGE 3 • 1000 HEADWORDS

… should, may – present perfect continuous – *used to* – past perfect – causative – relative clauses – indirect statements …

Of course, it was most important that no one should see Colin, Mary, or Dickon entering the secret garden. So Colin gave orders to the gardeners that they must all keep away from that part of the garden in future. *The Secret Garden*

STAGE 4 • 1400 HEADWORDS

*… past perfect continuous – passive (simple forms) –
would* conditional clauses – indirect questions –
relatives with *where/when* – gerunds after prepositions/phrases …

I was glad. Now Hyde could not show his face to the world again. If he did, every honest man in London would be proud to report him to the police. *Dr Jekyll and Mr Hyde*

STAGE 5 • 1800 HEADWORDS

… future continuous – future perfect –
passive (modals, continuous forms) –
would have conditional clauses – modals + perfect infinitive …

If he had spoken Estella's name, I would have hit him. I was so angry with him, and so depressed about my future, that I could not eat the breakfast. Instead I went straight to the old house. *Great Expectations*

STAGE 6 • 2500 HEADWORDS

… passive (infinitives, gerunds) – advanced modal meanings –
clauses of concession, condition

When I stepped up to the piano, I was confident. It was as if I knew that the prodigy side of me really did exist. And when I started to play, I was so caught up in how lovely I looked that I didn't worry how I would sound. *The Joy Luck Club*